ANCIENT EGYPTIANS

AN ANCIENT CIVILISATION BROUGHT VIVIDLY TO LIFE

BY FIONA MACDONALD

An imprint of HarperCollinsPublishers

Consultant: Dr Ian Shaw
Project Manager: Jilly MacLeod
Art Director: Rachel Hamdi
Picture Researcher: Cathie Arrington
Designer: Holly Mann
Cover Designer: James Annal
Editor: Julia Bruce

Ancient Egyptians accompanies the television series of the same name created by Wall to Wall for Channel Four, TLC ® and Granada International in association with Canal+, Norddeutscher Rundfunk/Germany, RAI - Radiotelevisione Italiana, Seven Network Australia and Warner Home Video Inc., A Warner Bros. Entertainment Company.

First published in 2003 by HarperCollins*Children's Books*, a division of HarperCollins*Publishers* Ltd, 77-85 Fulham Palace Road, London W6 8JB.
Text copyright © 2003 HarperCollins*Publishers*
Photographs by Giles Keyte copyright © Wall to Wall (Egypt) Ltd 2002
Cover photograph copyright © Wall to Wall (Egypt) Ltd 2002

wall to wall

The Wall to Wall website address is: www.walltowall.co.uk

The HarperCollins website address is: www.harpercollins.co.uk

ISBN: 0 00 715376 7

1 3 5 7 9 10 8 6 4 2

The author asserts the moral right to be identified as the author of this work.
A CIP record for this book is available from the British Library

Printed and bound in Belgium

CONTENTS

THE KINGDOM ON THE NILE

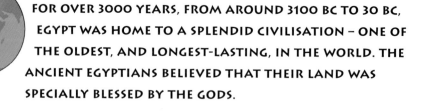

FOR OVER 3000 YEARS, FROM AROUND 3100 BC TO 30 BC, EGYPT WAS HOME TO A SPLENDID CIVILISATION – ONE OF THE OLDEST, AND LONGEST-LASTING, IN THE WORLD. THE ANCIENT EGYPTIANS BELIEVED THAT THEIR LAND WAS SPECIALLY BLESSED BY THE GODS.

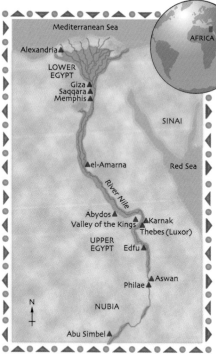

Above: The ancient Egyptians lived in settlements built on the banks of the Nile and in the marshy Delta region, where the Nile flows into the sea.

Below: Egypt's rulers wore magnificent jewels of gold and precious stones, like this scarab beetle good luck charm. The bright blue beetle is made of semi-precious lapis lazuli.

RED LAND, BLACK LAND

Egypt is situated in north Africa – a harsh, hot, dry region. The ancient Egyptians called it Deshret (the Red Land); we still use a modern form of this word – 'desert' – today. But a mighty river, the Nile, ran through the Egyptian desert, bringing life and prosperity to people living on its banks. Every year the Nile flooded, spreading a layer of sticky, smelly mud – which the Egyptians called 'Kemet' (the Black Land) – on either side.

Over 8000 years ago, Egyptian farmers discovered how to grow plentiful crops of wheat and barley in this black, fertile mud. They dug irrigation ditches to carry the Nile's floodwaters to new fields. Some thousand years later they domesticated (tamed) sheep, goats and cattle. By around 3500 BC they began building villages and tombs out of sun-dried mud bricks, and to mine gold and precious stones in the desert. They became rich, began to trade and built towns. They sent expeditions to the south to trade with lands in Africa, and to the north to fight against other powerful kingdoms in the Middle East.

RELIGIOUS IDEAS

The ancient Egyptians also developed powerful religious beliefs, which guided each part of their lives. For example, many settlements were built on the east bank of the Nile, the side where the sun rises, because ancient Egyptians believed that the rising sun was a sign of life. Tombs were built on the west bank of the river, where the sun sets – to the ancient Egyptians, this was the land of the dead.

Both men and women worshipped gods who reflected the world around them, such as Hapy, who brought the Nile

Right: A computer reconstruction of the great hypostyle hall (a hall with pillars) at the temple of the sun-god Amun at Karnak. The great pillars are portrayed here as open lotus flowers rising from swampy ground, representing both life and power.

Above: A tomb-painting shows a dead family (and their cat), happily catching river-birds in the idyllic afterlife. Living Egyptians also enjoyed hunting in the reedbeds beside the Nile.

floods or Nut, goddess of the starry sky. They also honoured animals such as scarabs (beetles), who arduously rolled balls of dung across the ground. This reminded them of the sun rolling across the sky every day, and made them think that scarabs had magic powers.

A NEW, STRONG KINGDOM

At first, Egypt was divided into two kingdoms, Upper Egypt, in the south, and Lower Egypt, in the north. But around 3100 BC, Upper and Lower Egypt were joined together. This united kingdom of Egypt was ruled by a very powerful king, later called a pharaoh. Over the centuries, Egypt grew richer and stronger. Pharaohs conquered new lands, built splendid palaces and paid for magnificent monuments, pyramids, temples and tombs. Egypt's hot, dry climate has preserved many of these treasures in excellent condition, and we can still wonder at them today.

DISCOVERING THE PAST

EGYPTIAN CIVILISATION HAS FASCINATED PEOPLE FOR THOUSANDS OF YEARS. THE FIRST CURIOUS VISITORS TO EGYPT CAME FROM ANCIENT GREECE AROUND 2500 YEARS AGO. TODAY, HISTORIANS, ARCHAEOLOGISTS, SCIENTISTS AND MANY OTHER SCHOLARS USE A WIDE RANGE OF TECHNIQUES TO INVESTIGATE ANCIENT EGYPT, AND BRING ITS AMAZING PAST TO LIFE.

WRITTEN RECORDS

One of the main sources of information about the ancient Egyptians is found in their own words. The Egyptians were one of the earliest people to invent a system of writing, and many ancient documents and inscriptions (texts carved on stone) have survived until today. These documents were created by professional writers, or scribes, using three different scripts.

Hieroglyphs (picture-symbols), invented around 3100 BC, are the oldest form of Egyptian writing. Each picture-symbol represented an object, an idea, or later a sound. They were used mostly for religious texts or to record important information, such as famous victories in battle.

After around 1780 BC, scribes began to use hieratic script for government records, scientific and medical works and books of magic spells. Hieratic was also based on picture-symbols, but combined them with shapes rather like

Above: These hieroglyphs, carved on the temple at Karnak, record a great Egyptian victory at the battle of Megiddo. You can read more about this on pages 56–57.

Below: Brief notes and messages were written and scratched on bits of stone or pieces of pottery called 'ostraca'.

letters. It was written on papyrus (paper made from reeds) with a reed pen and ink mixed from soot and water. Demotic script, invented around 500 BC, used flowing shapes instead of picture-symbols. It could be written very quickly, making it easy to use for hasty, scribbled note-taking.

STORIES IN PICTURES

Ancient Egyptians also left many clues about themselves in statues, carvings and wall-paintings. These supply details of their clothes, hairstyles, festivals and family life, and also their religious beliefs. All kinds of objects, from model farm animals buried in tombs to cooking pots and children's toys, also provide evidence of ancient Egyptians' everyday activities. But these clues all need to be interpreted with care, since the ancient

Below: Archaeologists can find out a great deal about the age, health, wealth, appearance and even cause of death from the mummified remains of ancient Egyptians.

RE-LIVING THE PAST

Stories, plays, films and TV programmes about the ancient Egyptians have been popular for many years. But more recently, television companies, aided by teams of experts, have recreated and filmed (right) actual events recorded in Egyptian texts. This has helped us discover how certain ancient tools and weapons worked, and to get a sense of what it might have been like to live in Egyptian times. Throughout this book, you can see photos of actors recreating real ancient Egyptian lives.

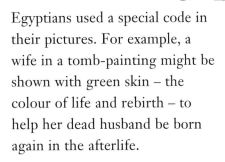

Egyptians used a special code in their pictures. For example, a wife in a tomb-painting might be shown with green skin – the colour of life and rebirth – to help her dead husband be born again in the afterlife.

BURIED TREASURES, NEW TECHNIQUES

For centuries, visitors to Egypt opened up tombs and dug in the desert in search of valuable items buried with the dead. Some amazing discoveries were made in this way, including Tutankhamun's tomb with all its treasures found in 1922. But early investigators often used intrusive techniques, such as unwrapping mummies, to

Right: Medical CAT (Computed Axial Tomography) scanners take pictures of cross-sections (like 'slices'), at 5 mm intervals. A computer then uses this data to create 3-D images, which can be viewed from any angle.

discover more. Today, scientists use less destructive methods. They examine mummies with medical scanners and endoscopes (tiny cameras at the end of flexible tubes). They use microscopes to magnify samples of mummy-flesh and computers to recreate faces from shrivelled skin and bones. They look for buried sites from the air – or even from space. Recently, space photos have revealed the tracks of irrigation ditches in the desert, forgotten for thousands of years.

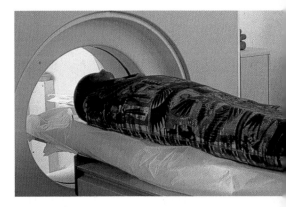

FROM PHARAOH TO FARMER

ACCORDING TO EGYPTIAN MYTH THE WORLD HAD BEEN CREATED BY THE GODS AND WAS RESTORED EACH DAY BY THE SUN. ANCIENT EGYPTIANS BELIEVED THAT THEY HAD A PART TO PLAY IN KEEPING THE WORLD ALIVE, BY CARRYING OUT THE PROPER DUTIES FOR THEIR RANK IN SOCIETY AS PHARAOH, PRIEST OR FARMER.

SUPERHUMAN

Pharaohs were not like ordinary men. They were superhuman 'sons of the sky'. Their mothers 'married' the sun-god in magic ceremonies before they were born. In Egyptian eyes, this gave them god-like authority, and also special responsibilities. As high priest, for instance, the king served as a living link between people and gods, while as army commander he had to defend Egypt from all enemies.

GOVERNMENT BUSINESS

A primary duty of the pharaoh was to ensure the country was efficiently run. Government business was organised by the Vizier (prime minister) and Overseer of Works. There were also local officials – district governors and town mayors – who all relied on skilled scribes to issue orders and instructions, collect taxes, draft laws, manage construction projects and keep government records.

Above: According to Egyptian myths, Hathor, 'lady of the sky' and goddess of music and pleasure, was the magical mother and protector of each ruling pharaoh.

PAID TO PRAY

The Egyptians thought that if the gods were offended or ignored the world would come to an end, so pharaohs employed many priests and priestesses to say prayers and make offerings in the temples to please the gods. Priests might also act as government advisers, or manage large estates belonging to the temples where they worked. At times, they caused considerable controversy by meddling in politics.

Left: To show their special status, pharaohs wore several different crowns. This gold band is decorated with a *uraeus* symbolising Wadjyt, the snake-goddess, ready to strike and kill Egypt's enemies.

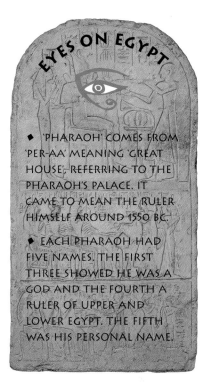

Left: A senior priest, wearing a leopard-skin over a fine linen robe. Priests were not allowed to wear leather or wool, which were regarded as ritually unclean.

ORDINARY LIVES

There was an enormous gap, in both rank and wealth, between pharaohs, priests and scribes and ordinary working people. Most men and women in Egypt were poor, and had little or no power. Their short lives – very few survived above 40 years – were spent working hard and obeying orders.

Most ordinary people were farmers, who grew crops to feed their families and to pay the rent and taxes demanded by pharaohs. Some men earned a living by sailing boats or catching fish on the River Nile; others quarried rock or mined gold and precious stones. Women cared for their homes and families. They also wove cloth, baked bread and brewed beer. In towns, there were enterprising traders and groups of skilled craftworkers, such as potters, jewellers and carpenters. These all made more money than ordinary farmers or labourers and could afford larger houses, better food and finer clothes and belongings.

Some Egyptian citizens were slaves, often prisoners of war, captured by Egyptian soldiers and sold to the highest bidder. But slaves were usually well treated. They could own property, marry whom they chose and were often freed when their master or mistress died.

EYES ON EGYPT

• 'PHARAOH' COMES FROM 'PER-AA' MEANING 'GREAT HOUSE', REFERRING TO THE PHARAOH'S PALACE. IT CAME TO MEAN THE RULER HIMSELF AROUND 1550 BC.

• EACH PHARAOH HAD FIVE NAMES. THE FIRST THREE SHOWED HE WAS A GOD AND THE FOURTH A RULER OF UPPER AND LOWER EGYPT. THE FIFTH WAS HIS PERSONAL NAME.

Below: A wealthy husband and wife. Women in ancient Egypt had many legal rights; they could own property, run businesses, make wills, take legal action and speak in court – all without male permission.

Left: A farmer and his family carry sheaves of grain home from the fields at harvest time. Egyptian families were close and each member was expected to do their share of hard work.

FAMOUS PHARAOHS

WE KNOW OF OVER 300 PHARAOHS WHO RULED EGYPT BETWEEN 3100 BC AND 30 BC. WHILE THEY LIVED, THEIR NAMES WERE PRAISED, RESPECTED AND SOMETIMES HATED OR FEARED THROUGHOUT NORTH AFRICA AND THE MIDDLE EAST. BUT ONLY A FEW HAVE REMAINED FAMOUS UNTIL TODAY. WHY DO WE REMEMBER THEM?

Above: Tutankhamun (ruled 1334–1325 BC) died when he was just 18 years old. Even so, his tomb contained some of the finest treasures ever made in ancient Egypt.

WARRIORS

Some pharaohs were renowned for being great war-leaders, increasing Egypt's wealth and power by conquering new lands. Amenhotep I, who ruled from 1525–1504 BC, sent armies south to take control of Nubia (modern Sudan). Tuthmosis III (ruled 1479–1425 BC) marched north with his soldiers to defeat the Syrians. The strong defender Rameses II (ruled 1279–1213 BC) saved Egypt by opposing Hittite invaders from Asia Minor (modern Turkey), and forcing them to make peace.

GREAT BUILDERS

We remember other pharaohs for the buildings they left behind. The magnificent and mysterious pyramids, built to contain the tombs of Pharaoh Khufu (ruled 2589–2566 BC) and Pharaoh Khafra (ruled 2558–2532 BC) still inspire awe and wonder today.

Rameses II built over a dozen huge temples, including massive monuments such as the vast hypostyle hall, covering half a hectare, and the pylon (ceremonial gateway) at Karnak, near Thebes.

RULERS FROM OTHER LANDS

Traditionally, the right to be pharaoh passed from father to son, and Egypt's ruling dynasties (powerful families) jealously guarded their power. But a few famous pharaohs came from outside Egypt. They included Persian Emperor Cambyses and his descendants, who ruled from 525–404 BC. In 323 BC King Alexander the Great of Macedonia invaded Egypt.

GREAT ROYAL WIFE

Left: Queen Nefertari (lived c1300–1250 BC), Great Royal Wife of Rameses II, makes an offering of milk to the gods. Pharaohs had many wives, including foreign princesses and even, sometimes, their own sisters or daughters. The pharaoh's senior wife was given the title Great Royal Wife, and had important religious and ceremonial duties to perform. Most had little political power, but Nefertari was regarded highly by Rameses and many portraits show them side by side, as if they were joint rulers.

Left: Tuthmosis III (ruled 1479–1425 BC) salutes his subjects from a special 'window of appearances', high in his palace wall. Pharaohs stood at these windows to greet important foreign visitors and to hand out rewards.

Below: The face of Rameses II gazes down from a 20-metre high statue that confronts visitors to the great temple he built at Abu Simbel, in the far south of Egypt. As here, pharaohs were often portrayed wearing a false beard, a sign of godlike power.

His generals set up a new ruling dynasty, the Ptolemies. The fascinating queen Cleopatra VII (born 69 BC), last independent ruler of ancient Egypt, belonged to this foreign family. She ruled until 30 BC, when Egypt was finally conquered by Rome.

WOMEN WITH POWER

Pharaohs were nearly always men, but a few remarkable women also ruled Egypt, long before Cleopatra. Queen Ahhotep I (lived 1590–1530 BC) was the daughter, wife and mother of pharaohs. She governed Egypt while her son, Pharaoh Ahmose I, was away fighting battles, earning the title 'mistress of the land'.

About 1400 years earlier a woman called Merneith seems to have been appointed king, perhaps acting as regent until her son Den (ruled around 2950 BC) became old enough to rule in his own right. Similarly, in 1473 BC Queen Hatshepsut, widow of Pharaoh Tuthmosis II, was appointed regent (governor), because the rightful pharaoh, Tuthmosis III, was still a child. But when Tuthmosis grew up, Hatshepsut refused to hand over power. She had herself crowned pharaoh, ordered the building of a temple and tomb, sent trading expeditions to distant lands and began wars with Egypt's neighbours. Hatshepsut stayed in power until her death in 1458 BC, after which her name was removed from her funeral temple, as people believed it was wrong for a woman to rule.

HOMES OF THE GODS

TEMPLES WERE HOLY HOMES, BUILT TO SHELTER STATUES OF THE GODS AND TO RECEIVE THEIR SPIRITS. THEY WERE ALSO MONUMENTS TO DEAD PHARAOHS, AND PROUD, CONFIDENT PROOF OF EGYPT'S WEALTH, POWER AND CRAFTSMANSHIP. THE EGYPTIANS CALLED THEM 'HOUSES OF ETERNITY' AND HOPED THEY WOULD LAST FOR EVER.

Above: Rows of ram-headed monsters, called criosphinxes, guard the way to the great temple of the sun-god Amun, at Karnak. To the Egyptians, these were 'living images' of Amun, and symbols of his great power.

A SACRED SPACE

Temples were designed with a magical purpose – to recreate, in stone, the 'island of creation'. According to Egyptian myth, this was the first dry land to emerge from the sea at the beginning of the world. Like this wondrous island, temples rose high above their surroundings – usually, the flat, dry desert. Each was enclosed by a mud-brick wall, decorated with wavy lines that represented the waters surrounding the newly created land,

Below: This huge pylon (gateway) stood at the entrance to the inner courtyard of Amun's temple at Karnak. Only pharaohs, priests and temple servants could set foot on the holy ground inside.

long ago. They also separated the temple's sacred space from the rest of the everyday world.

Temples were laid out rather like an Egyptian house, but on a massive scale. Public rooms for visitors were at the front, private, or holy rooms were at the back. Temple visitors approached along ceremonial walkways before passing through the temple walls to outer, public courtyards. Entrance to the holiest inner rooms was barred by massive gateways called pylons. Ordinary people could not go inside.

TEMPLE CEREMONIES

All temple worship was performed by priests. Each day, they took part in elaborate rituals, accompanied by music, dancing and chanting. The Egyptians believed that these ceremonies were essential to keep the sun rising and the world running as it should.

At sunrise, priests purified themselves by washing in the

temple's sacred lake. Then they walked in procession through its inner halls, burning incense to create clouds of sweet-smelling smoke, and sprinkling water to drive all unholy influences away. Finally, they entered the sanctuary – the holiest room in the temple. The spirit of each god 'lived' here, in a beautiful, awe-inspiring statue, protected by a shrine decorated with precious stones. Every night, the doors of the shrine were closed and sealed with a disc of clay, so that the statue god could 'sleep'.

The following morning, with reverently bowed heads, priests approached the shrine, saying 'I am a pure one'. They broke the seal on the shrine doors and opened them to 'wake' the statue. Then, like servants caring for a living person, they washed the statue with holy water, and dressed it in beautiful clothes. Later in the day priests left food and drink in

Above: Rich, powerful people, like priest Petiese (see page 20) paid for mortuary temples with statues representing their own 'ka' (life-force), to be built close to their tombs.

front of the statue, to 'feed' the spirit it contained.

Women could serve as priests as well, especially in temples dedicated to a powerful goddess. They also sang and danced in temple rituals, chanting hymns of praise to the gods.

TEMPLES, TITHES AND TAXES

TEMPLES WERE AMONG THE BIGGEST, MOST BEAUTIFUL BUILDINGS IN EGYPT. THEY WERE COMMISSIONED BY PHARAOHS OR TOP OFFICIALS, CONSTRUCTED BY CONSCRIPTED (FORCED) LABOUR AND RUN BY PRIESTS AND SCRIBES. THEY WERE PAID FOR BY TAXES, AND SUPPORTED BY TITHES (SHARES OF PRODUCE) GIVEN TO THEM BY FAMILIES WHO LIVED AND WORKED ON TEMPLE FARMS.

SERVANTS OF THE PHARAOH

By law, every Egyptian was a servant of the pharaoh and had to work for him and pay taxes. During the Nile flood season, when farmland was too wet to cultivate, men – and occasionally women – were rounded up by royal officials, marched away from their villages and forced to labour on massive royal building projects such as temples, pyramids and irrigation schemes. In return, they were given food and shelter, but no wages.

Anyone trying to run away or avoid this work was punished by local magistrates. If they offended a second time they might be sent south to the gold mines in Nubia (Sudan) where the conditions were so bad that most miners died. Wealthy people paid large sums to avoid this work duty – an option not available to the poor.

Royal taxes were assessed by government officials. They visited farms to measure the fields and count the livestock. Normally, taxes were due at harvest time – and had to be paid, even if the harvest had failed and the farmer had no food to feed his family.

PAYMENT IN KIND

Because Egyptian people did not use coins until around 500 BC, they paid taxes 'in kind', that is by handing over to the tax collectors goods they had produced, such as grain, livestock, geese, honey and linen cloth. Anyone who was late paying, or who refused to pay, was severely beaten. Collectors were always accompanied by slaves carrying big sticks and wooden clubs.

Right: Smoke swirls around as incense is burnt to honour the golden statue of a god. The Egyptians imported frankincense, and other sweet-smelling resins (sticky sap from trees), from the land of Punt (probably present-day Eritrea).

Above: A tax collector counting geese. Royal officials visited farms every other year to check their records and calculate how much tax to collect.

TEMPLE TITHES

As well as owing tax and work-services to the pharaoh, most ordinary families also had to pay a kind of rent, or tithe, to their landlords. This was because they were 'meret' (unfree). They belonged to powerful landowners – rich families, or temples – and had to give them a share of the produce grown on their land. Each year, they carried the tithe they owed to granaries and storerooms on great estates where it was carefully recorded by scribes, who were themselves exempt from these tithes.

Egyptian priests claimed they had a right to this produce because they offered prayers in the temple and sacrifices to the gods on behalf of all Egyptian people. As a result, they were much better fed than ordinary men and women.

When the Greek geographer, Herodotus, visited Egypt around 500 BC, he observed this custom reporting, 'Priests don't have to provide their own food or pay for anything. Every day, they are given fresh bread baked from the temple's corn, and plenty of beef and roast goose.'

EYES ON EGYPT

● THE TEMPLE OF KARNAK IS THE LARGEST RELIGIOUS BUILDING IN THE WORLD. IT COVERS 81 HECTARES/ 200 ACRES AND TOOK 500 YEARS TO COMPLETE.

● THE TEMPLE CONTAINS THE BIGGEST SACRED LAKE IN EGYPT, MEASURING SOME 13,500 SQ M/1,453,126 SQ FT. STATUES OF THE GODS WERE SAILED ACROSS THE LAKE ON GOLDEN BARGES.

Below: Scribes making lists of goods paid to a temple as tithe. Scribes and priests did not pay taxes or tithes, since they did not grow crops or raise animals. Instead they provided a service to the pharaoh and the people.

MURDER IN THE TEMPLE

Above: Karem and Ibi, grandsons of government official Petiese. They were born into a powerful family and killed by jealous priests.

Below: Terrified, Karem and Ibi run for their lives as priests armed with heavy wooden clubs chase them across the temple courtyard.

Around 700 BC, Egypt was in danger. Nubians attacked from the south and Syrians advanced from the north. Pharaohs led armies to fight these invaders, leaving priests in charge of government tasks, such as collecting taxes and administering laws. The most powerful of the priests served Amun, the ram-headed guardian god. While the pharaohs were fighting, the priests took control of both the land and people.

In 664 BC, a new pharaoh, Psamtek I, came to power. He devoted the early years of his reign to driving out foreign invaders, but then had to face another problem – the priests of Amun had become too powerful. But he dared not anger them – Egypt would be ruined, if the priests decided to rebel.

This difficult situation left one of Psamtek's senior officials with a terrible choice between love and duty. The official's name was Petiese. His family's tragic story was recorded by scribes, and we can still read it today.

Petiese trained as a priest, but had become a loyal friend of the pharaoh. He worked to make sure that all provinces in Egypt obeyed the pharaoh's orders, and to stop temple priests gaining any more power. He lived in the rich city of Teudjoi, with his daughter Nitemhe, son-in law Horudj, and their two young sons, Karem and Ibi.

Petiese was rich. The pharaoh had given him the right to one fifth of all taxes paid to the temple in his city. This was twenty times more than any other

Above: Nitemhe collapses in shock and horror when her own father, Petiese, decides to let the men who killed her sons to go free.

priest. Every year, Petiese and his family received huge quantities of wheat, barley and other foods. They used some to eat, and others to barter for comfortable furniture and fine clothes and belongings. Petiese also paid for a handsome statue of himself to be placed in the temple sanctuary. All this made Petiese unpopular with the temple priests. They also hated Horudj, who was stupid, greedy and lazy. But the family was too powerful for the priests to overthrow them.

One day at harvest time, Petiese and Horudj were both away from home. So Nitemhe, Petiese's daughter, sent Karem and Ibi to the temple to collect the family's share of the grain-taxes, instead. Seeing that the boys were undefended, three young priests saw a way to get at Petiese and attacked and killed the boys.

When she heard the news, Nitemhe was distraught – and very scared. Would the priests try and kill her next? She barricaded herself inside her

house until Petiese hurried back. Helped by the local police, he tracked down the murderers, and put them on trial. They admitted their guilt and expected to die.

But then Petiese did a remarkable thing – he let them go free! Nitemhe was horrified; she could not understand why her father chose not to punish the men who killed her sons. Even the temple priests and local policemen were surprised. But the more they thought about it, the more they realised that Petiese had made a wise decision. Killing the murderous priests would not bring the dead boys back to life, but it might spark off a bitter war between priests and officials like Petiese, who administered the pharaoh's laws. If the citizens were to join in, this would destroy the peace and prosperity of their town and lead to more bloodshed. Petiese's wise decision averted any further conflict.

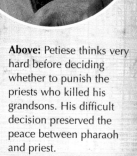

Above: Petiese thinks very hard before deciding whether to punish the priests who killed his grandsons. His difficult decision preserved the peace between pharaoh and priest.

Below: The young priests who killed Karem and Ibi kneel to hear Petiese's verdict. The usual Egyptian punishment for murder was death.

Gods and Goddesses

EGYPTIAN MEN AND WOMEN BELIEVED THAT GODS AND GODDESSES WATCHED OVER EVERYONE'S LIFE FROM THE MOMENT THEY WERE BORN TO THE TIME THEY WERE BURIED, AND THAT THEIR POWER CONTINUED INTO THE WORLD OF THE DEAD – THE AFTERLIFE. NOTHING WAS HIDDEN FROM THEM. THE GODS INSPIRED RESPECT, FEAR – AND LOVE.

Below: Amun was originally the main god of the city of Thebes. He became popular throughout Egypt, and was joined in people's minds with another great god, Re, lord of the sun. This new god, Amun-Re, became the most powerful god of all.

Above: Women prayed to Taweret, the hippopotamus goddess, to protect them in childbirth. She was usually portrayed with a very rounded belly, as if she was pregnant.

NATIONAL GODS

Egyptian people worshipped three different kinds of gods and goddesses. The most powerful were national gods, such as the great Osiris, 'he who never decays'. Osiris was lord of life, growth and fertility, guardian of the Nile floods and ruler of the next world. He was often portrayed in bandages, like a mummy, because he helped dead people to be re-born. Myths told how Osiris was murdered by his brother Seth, the god of chaos and darkness, who cut his body into pieces. The goddess Isis, who was Osiris's sister and wife, found the pieces and put them together again with the help of Anubis, the jackal-headed god of mummy-making. Using magic she brought Osiris back to life.

LOCAL HEROES

Each region of Egypt also had its own special, local gods. These were often closely linked to the local environment. For example, Sobek, the crocodile-god, was worshipped in the marshy Faiyum region, where many dangerous crocodiles lurked. These could kill or cause terrible injuries to anyone who got too close to them.

Some places became famous as centres of worship for their own, special gods.

For instance, Hathor, the cow-headed goddess of music and love, protected the land of the dead on the west bank of the Nile. She was principally worshipped in the cities of Thebes and Dendera where local people built splendid temples to honour her. You can see Hathor, peering through tall reeds on the bank of the Nile, behind the goddess Taweret in the papyrus painting opposite.

FAMILY FRIENDS

Egyptian families also prayed every day to friendly household gods, such as Bes, who was usually shown as a dwarf with a lion's mane and a sticking-out tongue. People kept statues of

Left: The goddess Isis 'great in magic' was honoured by the pharaohs as their mother. Here she is shown nursing her son, the hawk-god Horus in human form.

DAY AND NIGHT

Nut was the goddess of the starry night sky. The Egyptians pictured her as a beautiful woman bending over the earth. Myths told how every evening, she swallowed the setting sun (you can see the sun and its rays in Nut's outstretched arms, right). The next morning she gave birth to it again, bringing light and life back to the world.

him in their homes, or wore little images of him as lucky charms. Women honoured Taweret, goddess of childbirth, and Heket, the frog-goddess. She watched over families and shaped unborn babies in the womb. Men prayed to gods who protected their occupations, such as Onuris, who helped warriors. They also made offerings to placate Meretseger, a snake goddess, so that she would protect them from dangerous snakes as they worked on the building of tombs.

LIFE AND DEATH

Egyptian people believed that all their actions had a religious meaning, and might be judged accordingly. Gods and goddesses could send terrible punishments, such as blindness, to people who angered them or disturbed the good order of the world. Many were shown

carrying an 'ankh', a cross with a looped top, the symbol of life. This reminded the Egyptians that the gods gave life – but could also bring death. You can see an ankh in the goddess Taweret's left hand in the picture opposite.

Some gods and goddesses had multiple powers. Nut, the goddess of the sky and heavens, for instance, was also honoured at funerals. Her image was painted on the inside of mummy cases, and Egyptian people prayed to her, 'Mother Nut, spread yourself over me so that I may go to live among the everlasting stars, and never die.'

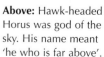

Above: Hawk-headed Horus was god of the sky. His name meant 'he who is far above'.

FESTIVALS AND OFFERINGS

ORDINARY MEN AND WOMEN WERE NOT ALLOWED INSIDE TEMPLES, BUT THEY DID GET A THRILLING CHANCE TO MEET THEIR GODS ON FESTIVAL DAYS. ON THESE OCCASIONS HOLY STATUES WERE CARRIED SHOULDER-HIGH TO THE FIELDS, OR ROWED ALONG THE RIVER, TO SPREAD BLESSINGS OVER EGYPT'S LAND AND PEOPLE.

SPLENDID OCCASIONS

There were five to ten festivals every month, depending on the season. The most important was Opet, held during the second month of the Nile floods (August to September), to honour the most important national god, Amun-Re, his wife Mut and their child Khonsu. The government declared an 11-day national holiday, and many families celebrated with parties and feasts.

Each festival was a splendid occasion. The statue of the god or goddess was placed in a sacred boat decorated with leaves, branches or flowers. Its face was veiled – to hide it from unholy public view – but onlookers could still catch a glimpse of its powerful torso and graceful limbs of painted clay, carved wood or smooth stone. Egyptians believed that their gods either looked like humans, but more perfect, or else like wild animals or birds: often dangerous, but at the same time, very beautiful and strong.

Priests carried the statue and fanned it with palm leaves or ostrich feathers, as if it were a pharaoh. They scented the air around it with incense and set it down from time to time to rest at kiosks (small temples), while they said prayers and made offerings.

At some festivals, ordinary men and women could approach the statue, and ask it to see into the future, or to solve difficult problems for them.

FESTIVAL FOODS

Festivals didn't just give the people a chance to feel close to the gods and to ask them for

Left: Many Egyptian homes contained painted clay statues of the god Bes, protector of women and young children. They were often placed in areas where women commonly worked, such as courtyards.

EYES ON EGYPT

• CARVINGS OF EARS ON TEMPLES' OUTER WALLS ALLOWED PEOPLE TO COMMUNICATE WITH THE GODS WITHOUT ENTERING.

• WOMEN PILGRIMS SAILING DOWN THE NILE TO CELEBRATE THE FESTIVAL OF CAT-HEADED GODDESS BASTET, GOT DRUNK, SANG, DANCED AND EXPOSED THEIR PRIVATE PARTS TO VILLAGERS AS THEY PASSED BY!

help, they were also valued for another reason. At festival times, priests from temples shared rich offerings of food and drink with crowds of ordinary people. The Egyptians liked to please their gods by giving them gifts of many good things, such as fresh flowers, corn, vegetables, honey, spices, cakes and beer. Small 'samples' of these were placed in front of gods' statues, and the rest was kept in temple storerooms, to be handed out at festival time. Festivals were often the only chance that poor people had to eat meat – which was normally very expensive. In addition, drunkenness at festivals was encouraged, as a way of honouring the gods.

RELIGIOUS DRAMA

At some festivals, priests and priestesses acted out Egyptian myths that described the lives of gods or goddesses in front of a large audience of ordinary people. These performances were part entertainment, part worship, and very popular with Egyptian crowds.

FAVOURITE GODS

If they could afford it, Egyptians also liked to make pilgrimages to take part in festivals held at towns where their favourite god or goddess was worshipped. They often purchased special offerings, such as mummies of sacred birds and animals, to leave at their temples and shrines.

Left: Worshippers of the cat goddess, Bastet, left thousands of mummified cats as offerings at her temple at Bubastis, in northern Egypt.

Below: Egyptians believed that the popular snake goddess, Renenutet, 'lady of the granaries' protected their food-stores from mice and other pests. They left offerings and made 'bowers' of leaves, reeds and grains where Renenutet could hide.

EVERLASTING LIFE

THE ANCIENT EGYPTIANS BELIEVED THAT EVERY MAN, WOMAN AND CHILD HAD A UNIQUE LIFE FORCE, CALLED A 'KA'. IT WAS CREATED THE MOMENT A PERSON WAS BORN AND COULD GO ON LIVING AFTER THEY DIED – AS LONG AS IT WAS PROPERLY CARED FOR. SKILLED WORKERS PRESERVED DEAD BODIES BY MAKING THEM INTO MUMMIES. THIS PROVIDED EACH KA WITH A HOME.

MUMMIFICATION

Mummy-makers, or embalmers, used many techniques to prevent dead bodies decaying. First they washed the corpse and removed its internal organs, which would otherwise rot very quickly in Egypt's hot sun. To do this, they made a cut about 10 cm long near the left hip, then pulled out the lungs, liver, stomach and intestines. These were preserved in natron, a type of salt that absorbs water, and stored in special containers called canopic jars which were buried alongside the mummy. Body parts were never thrown away in case magicians got hold of them and used them to cast evil spells.

The embalmers drained the body of blood, then removed the brain by forcing a strong metal hook through the thin bone at the back of the nose. By cleverly manipulating the hook, the brain could be pulled out of the skull through the nostrils. They left the heart because they believed it was used for thinking and would be needed in the afterlife!

Next, embalmers dried out the remaining flesh and bones, a long, expensive process, taking up to 70 days. Rich people paid more for their bodies to be dried thoroughly and to be coated in precious herbs and spices. They hoped this would give them extra years in the afterlife.

Above: Embalmers wash a newly removed organ before preserving it in natron. They would also wash out the empty body and pack it with natron. Then they would cover the body with more natron and leave it to dry out.

Right: Mummies were placed in body-shaped cases which provided a home for the ka. They were decorated with ritual verses and magic spells. A false beard – symbol of the god Osiris who rose from the dead – was often added as a sign of everlasting life.

A MAGIC GUIDE

Many mummies were buried with a 'Book of the Dead'. This was a collection of magic spells and prayers, written on papyrus and illustrated with pictures of gods, demons and monsters. It was designed to help the dead person's ka survive in the afterlife. It contained a guide to the dangerous journey the ka must make before reaching a peaceful resting place, called the Field of Reeds. It also told people how to speak to all the supernatural beings they might meet along the way.

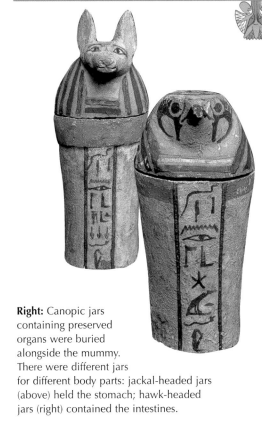

Right: Canopic jars containing preserved organs were buried alongside the mummy. There were different jars for different body parts: jackal-headed jars (above) held the stomach; hawk-headed jars (right) contained the intestines.

SHAPING UP

When the body was completely dried out, the embalmers arranged it into a life-like shape, holding the limbs in place with linen bandages soaked in resin (plant gum). The term 'mummy' comes from the Arabic word 'mummiya' meaning a dark, sticky tar. To make the withered flesh look more life-like, they plumped it up where necessary with pads of cloth. They filled the eye sockets with cloth, too, and sewed up the eyelids – because the chemical used to dry the body dissolved the eyeballs!

Next, the mummy was coated in resin and its face decorated with make-up. Finally, the mummy-makers wrapped it in hundreds of metres of linen bandages, placing magic amulets, or charms, between each layer to protect the body in the afterlife.

THE BEAUTIFUL HOUSE

Mummies were made in a special building called the 'beautiful house'. This name described the building's purpose – preparing a person for everlasting life – rather than its appearance or smell. In reality it must have reeked of decaying flesh, been spattered with blood and crawling with flies!

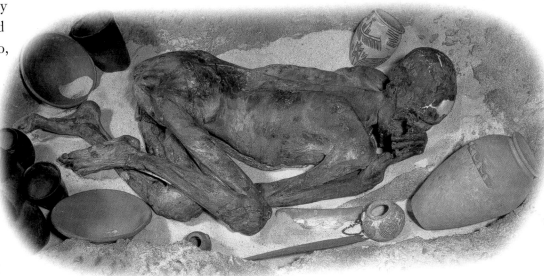

Right: This Egyptian man became a mummy about 5000 years ago. His family buried him in a sleeping position with a few treasured possessions close by, and his body dried out naturally in the hot, dry desert ground.

RITUALS OF DEATH

EGYPTIAN FUNERALS HELPED A DEAD PERSON'S KA (LIFE-FORCE) FIND ITS WAY FROM THIS WORLD TO THE NEXT. BUT THEY HAD TO BE PROPERLY PERFORMED. FRIENDS AND RELATIVES ALL NEEDED TO SAY THE RIGHT PRAYERS, CARRY OUT THE CORRECT RITUALS AND MAKE SUITABLE OFFERINGS AT THE DEAD PERSON'S TOMB.

A SPLENDID OCCASION

The grandest funerals were reserved for rich and powerful people such as pharaohs, or for holy animals that had been worshipped at temples and shrines. Poor people had much simpler funerals but with similar rituals and prayers. A royal funeral was a magnificent affair, and took months to organise.

When the dead pharaoh's mummy was ready for burial, it was placed in a decorated coffin and loaded on to a wooden sled. Often, this was boat-shaped. The Egyptians believed that pharaohs travelled through the afterlife on 'solar barks' (heavenly boats), like the sun or moon sailing across the sky. Gangs of strong men hauled the sled, while crowds of women mourners, playing musical instruments or wailing, tearing their clothes and pulling their hair, walked alongside.

As the procession approached the burial chamber, priests said prayers, burned incense and poured milk on the ground as an offering to the gods. Then came the most important ceremony of all called 'the opening of the mouth' which

Above: The 'opening of the mouth' ceremony. The mummy was placed upright. Then close relatives or priests touched its ears, eyes and mouth with magical tools. Now its ka could hear, see and speak once more!

helped the dead person's ka return to the mummified body so that it could function normally in the afterlife.

LAID TO REST

The coffin was laid in the tomb with magic amulets and all the things the pharaoh might need in the Next World, such as food, clothes, jewellery, furniture and musical instruments.

Finally, priests sealed the tomb with a heavy slab of wood or stone representing a door leading from the world of the living to that of the dead. Egyptians believed a person's ka could pass through it, so they left offerings of food and drink close by, along with a statue of the pharaoh as he looked in life.

Left: Boxes of shabtis (little wooden or pottery figures) were placed in many tombs. Egyptians thought that the dead would have to work in the afterlife. As pharaohs and other powerful people were too important to work, they were given shabtis to do it for them.

The mummy of a sacred animal – the Apis Bull – is carried in procession along the Sacred Way that leads from the lively city of Memphis to the necropolis (city of the dead) at Saqqara. There it will be placed in a massive sarcophagus (stone coffin) and buried deep underground.

THE TWINS

Above: The sad tale of Taous and Tages is now known through the letters they wrote.

Below: The twins lead a procession of mourners through the streets. The women are dressed in drab blue and grey clothes to show their sadness, and have matted, uncombed hair. Their faces are streaked with white ash, and their eyes are rimmed with a black cosmetic called kohl.

In 164 AD, when their story begins, Taous and Tages were about 15 years old. They lived in a comfortable home in the city of Memphis with their parents, sister and stepbrother. Their father, Argynoutis, was respected but old and rather dull. Their mother, Nephoris, was young, beautiful – and ambitious!

At that time, Greek kings ruled Egypt, and Greek words, ideas, clothes and buildings were all very fashionable. Greek troops were also stationed in Egypt, to govern the country. Nephoris fell in love with a Greek soldier named Philippos. Together, they plotted to kill Argynoutis and steal all his money – including the share the twins should have received when they married.

Above: Driven by his desire to win the twins' mother – and their father's money – Greek soldier Philippos lashes out with his sword.

One night, Philippos attacked Argynoutis with his sword, then tried to drown him. (Argynoutis initially survived, but died shortly afterwards). The next day, Nephoris and Philippos turned the twins out of the family home.

Homeless, orphaned and penniless, the twins were in great danger. Where would they sleep? What would they eat? How could they survive? In desperation, they decided to make their way to the holy city of Saqqara, on the edge of the desert about 5 km away. A trusted friend of their father's lived there. Maybe he could help them! At Saqqara, to

their great relief, the twins found their father's friend, Ptolemaios. He worked in one of the temples as an Interpreter of Dreams. All Egyptians believed that dreams were important – they could heal, cure sickness or carry messages from the gods. Ptolemaios greeted the twins kindly but could do little to help them. He was not rich – and he was not free. As a temple servant he was bound to work in the confines of the temple for the rest of his life. He received food and lodgings but could never leave.

It seemed that the twins had only two choices. They could either work as temple servants, like Ptolemaios, or become temple prostitutes. Both prospects seemed horrible. But then Ptolemaios heard exciting news. The Apis Bull had died! Egyptians believed that the Apis Bull was the god Ptah in animal shape. When it died, the whole nation mourned for 70 days. Its body was mummified like a pharaoh's, then buried with splendid ceremonies. Ptolemaios explained that, according to custom, twin girls would be needed to act the part of the goddesses Isis and Nephthys at its burial, and then to serve in its funeral temple.

The twins got the job! But it was exhausting work, weeping and wailing, and leading mournful processions. However, serving in the temple was not too bad, and the twins were well-paid, with generous bonuses. They planned to live comfortably together, and save for a happier future. Yet once again they were to be cruelly disappointed.

Nephoris, their mother, sent their stepbrother to visit them – and he stole all their savings. The last we hear from the twins is their letter to King Ptolemy VI, asking for help to recover their stolen property. From the evidence of another letter, we know that Tages was alive four years later, but that the writer was 'sick with worry' about her. After this final mention, the twins vanish from history – for ever.

Above: Playing the part of goddesses Isis and Nephthys, the twins are carried shoulder-high in a grand funeral procession that leads the Apis Bull's mummy to its tomb (see page 29) before the mummy is placed inside a massive coffin, carved from a single block of stone.

Left: The Apis Bull was the most sacred animal in Egypt. It was worshipped as the living image of the powerful god Ptah.

TOMBS IN THE DESERT

THE EGYPTIANS LOVED LIFE. FROM ALL THE EVIDENCE THEY LEFT BEHIND THEM, IT IS CLEAR THAT THEY ENJOYED FOOD, DRINK, MUSIC, DANCING, SPORTS AND GAMES. THEY HOPED FOR A HAPPY MARRIAGE AND MANY CHILDREN. BUT THEY KNEW THAT THEIR LIVES MIGHT END AT ANY TIME – IN AN ACCIDENT, IN WAR, OR DISEASE – SO THEY TOOK GREAT CARE TO MAKE PREPARATIONS FOR THE NEXT LIFE, AFTER DEATH.

EYES ON EGYPT

- THE BIGGEST PYRAMID TOMB IS THE GREAT PYRAMID AT GIZA. IT IS ALMOST 47M HIGH, AND ITS BASE MEASURES 53,000 SQ M.

- THE GREAT PYRAMID CONTAINS 3,200,000 BLOCKS OF STONE. EACH WEIGHS ABOUT 2.5 TONNES.

- THE WORD 'PYRAMID' COMES FROM THE NAME OF LITTLE MOUND-SHAPED CAKES, OFTEN LEFT AS OFFERINGS AT TEMPLES.

IN THE NEXT WORLD

In Egyptian eyes, death was simply an interruption to their continued existence in the afterlife. They believed that the next world was much like the world of the living – but better. In it, men and women would need everything that they had found necessary while they were alive, including a house, clothes and food. They built tombs to make sure they would not be homeless in the next world, and filled them with favourite – and useful – items such as clothes, food, furniture, musical instruments and games. Often, these were decorated with holy or magical designs. The Egyptians hoped this would help the dead person in the tomb to be re-born and enjoy a renewed existence in the afterlife.

AN ETERNAL HOME

The size and splendour of tombs varied just as much as the houses people lived in while alive. Poor people could only afford simple tombs – plain mud-brick shelters in communal cemeteries, built close to villages and towns but on the opposite side of the river. Cemeteries were usually in the desert, where the dry soil helped to preserve bodies. They became known by the Greek name, 'necropolis' – 'city of the dead'.

The very poorest families could not afford a place in the cemeteries, but buried their dead under the floors of their houses,

Above: Skilled artists decorate the walls of rock-cut tombs with paintings showing the dead person's journey through to the next world.

Right: The pyramids at Giza were built between 2589–2503 BC to house three pharaohs' tombs. The pyramids were originally covered with brilliant white limestone topped by shining gold.

Left: The entrance to a rock-cut tomb near the Valley of the Kings is marked by a small pyramid. The most famous of the 62 royal tombs found in the valley so far is that of Pharaoh Tutankhamun, buried in 1327 BC.

or courtyards. This made sure that the dead body was protected, and its spirit had a home.

THE FIRST PYRAMIDS

In complete contrast, Egyptian pharaohs, top government officials and wealthy families constructed some of the most magnificent funerary monuments ever seen. The largest, and most impressive, were the pyramids, first built about 2686 BC. Their extraordinary shape developed, over the centuries, from earlier box-shaped brick tombs, called 'mastabas'. These had wide bases, and inward-sloping sides. Originally, they were just one storey high, but wealthy families began to build them taller and taller, creating low pyramids with stepped sides.

VALLEY OF THE KINGS

After around 1550 BC, fashions in burials changed. Pharaohs and other important people began to be buried either in tombs shaped like miniature Egyptian temples or in chambers tunnelled deep into rocky hillsides. In areas where the terrain was suitable, like the Valley of the Kings and the Valley of the Queens, near Thebes, there were hundreds of burials. So many people were needed that a whole new village, called Deir el-Medina, was built to house the families of the builders, carpenters, masons, painters and other craftsmen who laboured to create the magnificent tombs.

BURIED TREASURE

PHARAOHS AND OTHER HIGH RANKING EGYPTIANS LIVED A LIFE OF LUXURY IN SUMPTUOUS PALACES SURROUNDED BY MAGNIFICENT GARDENS. THEIR CLOTHES WERE MADE OF THE FINEST LINEN AND THEY WORE JEWELS OF TURQUOISE AND DEEP-BLUE LAPIS LAZULI. IT IS NOT SURPRISING, THEREFORE, THAT THEIR TOMBS WERE ALSO FILLED WITH TREASURES, READY FOR THE NEXT LIFE.

Above: Everyday items made of valuable materials, such as this gold and enamel fan handle found in Tutankhamun's tomb, were buried with royal mummies for the dead pharaohs to use in the Next World.

COVERED IN GOLD

Some of the most valuable treasures covered the bodies of the dead. Jewelled portrait masks were placed over the face, to help identify the deceased pharaoh in the Next World. Coffins covered with gold foil guarded his fragile mummy. The rest of the burial chamber was stacked with expensive furniture, sweet-smelling incense and perfume, glass and weapons, and clothes and jewels for the re-born pharaoh to wear.

FIELD OF REEDS

Egyptian people hoped that their ka (spirit) would find a happy and peaceful new home in the Field of Reeds after death. A productive farm, a nice house, garden and access to water, plus a loving family, were the Egyptians' idea of heaven, so they painted the walls of their tombs with pictures to show how pleasant their future in the Field of Reeds might be. These pictures also had a magic purpose – to help create the life after death that Egyptians wished to enjoy.

A TEMPTING TARGET

All these treasures made burial places a favourite target for tomb–robbers. Egyptian priests warned that thieves would be cursed and punished by the gods. Tomb-builders made heavy wood or stone doors to try and stop anyone entering. And many ordinary people believed that the snake-goddess Meretseger slithered among royal tombs in the Valley of the Kings, ready to strike down intruders with her venom. But despite these warnings almost all the most important tombs were plundered soon after they were completed.

PRICELESS DATA

Today, we value the items buried in tombs for a different reason. They tell us a great deal about how ancient Egyptians lived, and what they believed. Modern archaeologists curse the tomb-robbers of today and in the past, for destroying valuable evidence!

Right: This gold panel from Pharaoh Tutankhamun's tomb shows his wife, Queen Ankhesenamun, spreading precious perfume on his chest. They are wearing jewelled collars and clothes made of delicate linen cloth.

TOMB ROBBERS

Above: Amenpanufer was tempted to commit crimes because his family was poor and hungry.

Below: Hurriedly, the robbers lift a royal mummy in its golden case out of a sarcophagus (stone coffin).

Between 1504 BC and 1069 BC, the bodies of dead pharaohs were buried deep in the rocky hillside of the Valley of the Kings. The entrances to their tombs were sealed by massive boulders or huge stone slabs. Inside, there were false doors, twisting corridors, dead ends and sudden drops in floor-level. Prayers, charms and curses gave magical protection, and special security guards, from Nubia, called the Medjay, patrolled the site.

Yet, in spite of these precautions, almost all royal tombs were robbed – even though, to most Egyptians, this was a truly terrible crime. They felt sure that damaging a pharaoh's body and disturbing his tomb would end his life among the gods in the Next World and bring chaos and destruction to Egypt and its people. So why was tomb-robbery so common?

Records surviving from the trial of one man, Amenpanufer, written in 1116 BC, help explain why – and how – tomb-robbery happened. Amenpanufer was a poor man, employed as a labourer in the quarries outside Thebes – a city close to the Valley of the Kings. His work was hard and he was not well paid, but he had a wife and four young children to support. Sometimes, he could not afford to buy food for them to eat.

There were many other poor people in Thebes. Ever since the pharaohs moved their royal court away around 1300 BC, the city had been suffering. Years of bad harvests led to an economic crisis.

Above: In the Great Temple of Karnak, officials wait for Amenpanufer's trial to begin.

Streets and houses were dirty, noisy, crowded, and badly in need of repair. City officials were corrupt, and could be bribed to ignore most crimes. There were merchants and rich citizens keen to buy cut-price, stolen treasures, with no questions asked!

Amenpanufer joined a gang of eight other robbers. They included a mason, two carpenters, and a labourer – all useful tomb-robbing skills – plus a boatman to row them across the River Nile. In his evidence to the court, Amenpanufer described how they forced their way into tombs, using wooden or copper tools, or lit a fire against the tomb wall and then threw water over it. The sudden change in temperature made the rock crack and shatter.

Once the robbers were inside a tomb, they lit candles to explore. Then, working quickly, they grabbed all the small, portable objects they could find. They smashed stone coffins and set fire to wooden mummy-cases to melt the gold that covered them. They even unwrapped mummy-bandages to get at the magic amulets inside.

Amenpanufer had been arrested for tomb-robbery once before. But he had paid a bribe, and been set free. But in 1116 BC Thebes' city leaders discovered that teams of expert tomb-builders and painters working in the Valley of the Kings were also robbing tombs. They rounded up all past suspects, including Amenpanufer.

This time, there was no escape. The trial was conducted by the Vizier – the pharaoh's chief law officer. He decided that Amenpanufer was guilty, along with other members of the gang. They were all sentenced to death. To make the punishment fit the crime, they were also told that their bodies would never be buried, so they would have no chance of reaching the Next World.

Above: As Amenpanufer is arrested, his wife clings to him, sobbing hysterically. She knows she may never see him alive again.

Below: Battered and bruised from torture in prison, Amenpanufer tells the Vizier how many people in Thebes are involved in tomb robbery. But this speech still does not save his life.

Law and order

COMMITTING A CRIME IN ANCIENT EGYPT WAS A DESPERATE AND DANGEROUS ACT. CRIMINALS RISKED THEIR HOMES, JOBS, FAMILIES – AND LIVES – IF THEY WERE CAUGHT. EVEN WORSE, THEY WOULD BE JUDGED IN THE NEXT LIFE. EGYPTIANS ALSO BELIEVED THAT EACH PERSON'S ACTIONS, GOOD OR BAD, AFFECTED THE 'GOOD ORDER' OF THE WHOLE WORLD.

Below: Finished documents were often stamped with seals shaped like scarab beetles. The underside was carved with hieroglyphs recording the name of the scribe or his master. The stamp was then inked and pressed on to the document.

JUDGEMENT DAY

Law and order throughout the universe were governed by the goddess Maat. You can see her seated on top of the scales in the picture on page 39. She controlled the seasons and the movement of stars in the sky, as well as setting the rules for people's good behaviour. If men and women disobeyed these rules they would be punished in this life by the law, or by natural disasters. Egyptians believed that they also faced a terrible fate in the next world. Maat judged their conduct by weighing their hearts against a feather, the symbol of truth. If they failed this test a terrible monster called Ammut, part lion, part hippopotamus and part crocodile, would gobble up their heart, and they would cease to be.

VIZIERS AND SCRIBES

The pharaoh was the chief priest of Maat, and it was his duty to maintain the law. He handed over

Left: Notaries (scribes learned in the law) worked in big cities and towns. People involved in legal disputes – usually over financial matters or inheritance – asked them for advice.

this responsibility to the Vizier, his chief minister. The Vizier acted as judge in the most important trials, and was also meant to make sure that the whole system of justice was run fairly. Scribes working for the Vizier recorded judgements made by courts and punishments handed down to convicted offenders. Records of past trials were stored for future consultation in the Vizier's office.

IN COURT

There were two kinds of courts in Egypt. The high courts tried people accused of serious crimes such as murder, assault and tomb-robbery. These were presided over by important judges. Local courts dealt with lesser crimes, such as petty theft or quarrels over land. There was no jury and no lawyers. A team of judges listened to arguments from the accusers and the accused, then they gave their verdict. Their word was law!

Above: Wooden shackles fasten a prisoner's hands behind his back. A stick was sometimes pushed through the shackle and twisted, causing terrible pain and even breaking bones.

TERRIBLE PUNISHMENTS

People accused of a crime were put in prison until it was time for their case to be heard. Judges often used torture to get information from suspects; their families might be tortured as well. Punishments for convicted criminals were also very cruel. They could be caned, or even branded with red-hot metal. This scarred their skin and marked them out as an offender for life.

They might be sent to brutal work camps, where they were forced to work until they dropped, sawing timber or quarrying stone. Or they might be exiled to Nubia, or a remote oasis in the desert, and be isolated for ever from their families and friends.

For the worst crimes, offenders might be punished by having their hand, nose or ears cut off. This was not only painful and disfiguring, but also often led to serious infections, which could kill them. For murder, judges could ask the pharaoh to impose the death penalty – by beheading, drowning or burning alive. These capital punishments were doubly dreadful to Egyptians. If their bodies were badly damaged during the execution, or left unburied, they believed they could have no life after death.

Below: Anubis (kneeling) checks the scales as the heart of a dead man is weighed against 'the feather of truth'. Maat looks on from the top of the scales, and the bird-headed scribe-god, Thoth, records the result.

CITY LIVING

EGYPTIAN CITIES WERE LARGE AND SPLENDID, WITH HUGE ROYAL
PALACES, IMPOSING GOVERNMENT OFFICES, BEAUTIFUL TEMPLES,
BUSY LAW-COURTS, SCHOOLS, WORKSHOPS AND MARKETS, ALL
CROWDED INSIDE STRONG DEFENSIVE WALLS. BUT THERE WAS
ANOTHER, LESS GLAMOROUS, SIDE TO CITY LIFE. BECAUSE THERE
WERE NO SEWERS, DRAINS OR RUBBISH COLLECTIONS, CITIES WERE
ALSO DIRTY, SMELLY AND SWARMING WITH RATS AND FLIES.

Above: Men at work on a building
site. Most Egyptian homes, from
palaces to workers' hovels, were made
of mud-brick. Mud was mixed with
water and chopped straw, then poured
into moulds and left out in the hot sun
to dry and bake hard.

CAPITAL EVIDENCE

Egypt had two capital cities –
first Memphis near present-day
Cairo, then Thebes near present-
day Luxor. There were also many
smaller cities and towns, about
which we know less than we
should like because their remains
are buried under modern
settlements. Around 1350 BC,
Pharaoh Akhenaten gave orders
for a new capital city to be built
at Tell el-Amarna, about halfway
between Memphis and Thebes. It
was deserted soon after his death
in 1336 BC, but its ruins survive,
giving a picture of one city's life.

Amarna was specially designed
for the pharaoh, so it tells us
what he and his architects
thought the ideal city should be
like. It was planned with separate
districts for the royal family,
senior officials, skilled workers
and ordinary labourers. A great
temple, dedicated to Akhenaten's
favourite god Aten (the sun-disk)
stood at the heart of the city, and
a burial place with rock-cut
tombs was planned, but left
unfinished, not far away.

COMFORT AND LUXURY

At Amarna, the homes of the rich
and powerful were comfortable
and luxurious. The largest had
over 20 rooms, including grand
reception rooms for welcoming
important visitors and bedrooms
with en-suite bathrooms. These
homes were sheltered from the
city's noise and bustle by
carefully tended gardens

Above: The great city of Thebes
began as a small, sleepy town. But
after around 2181 BC, powerful
pharaohs made it their home base.
As Egypt's capital, Thebes grew rich
and strong, and presented an imposing
frontage along the River Nile.

and thick, mud-brick walls. Labourers lived in much smaller houses. Typically, each family home had just three rooms – a living area, a bedroom and a kitchen – all crammed into a plot measuring no more than 5 x 10 metres. The bedroom was also used for storage, while the roof and the porch provided a little extra space for sleeping or sitting in the shade.

URBAN SPRAWL

Other cities, such as Memphis or Thebes, were not so neatly planned. Because building space inside city walls was limited, houses were often built side by side, in terraces, without a garden or even a back yard. Many were several storeys high. They had few windows, and must have been dark and rather airless inside. Both men and women spent as much time as they could out of doors, or working in the front rooms of their houses that opened on to the streets.

Rich people's city homes were larger, and sometimes even had gardens, but the land beyond their garden walls was often filled with a sprawl of smaller, poorer, homes. Streets could be dark, dirty and narrow. They were laid out haphazardly, without any overall plan. It must have been very difficult for strangers to find their way around!

Below: Many priests, scribes and other royal officials lived and worked in cities. This lifelike wooden statue portrays the priest Ka-aper, who lived around 2500 BC. To the Egyptians, his stout, well-built figure was a sign of high status, and the long cane he is holding was a symbol of authority.

LIVING OFF THE LAND

THE EGYPTIANS RELIED ON FARMING TO SURVIVE. IT WAS SO IMPORTANT THAT THEY NAMED THE MONTHS OF THEIR CALENDAR AFTER FARMING ACTIVITIES. THEY ALSO DESCRIBED THEIR IDEA OF HEAVEN - THE FIELD OF REEDS - AS A PEACEFUL, PRODUCTIVE FARM, WHERE CROPS AND ANIMALS GREW STRONG AND HEALTHY, TREES GAVE DELICIOUS FRUIT AND FISH SPLASHED IN SHALLOW POOLS.

Below: Harvesting grain. Ripe ears of wheat and barley are cut from the stalks with a sickle – a curved knife fitted with sharp flint blades – before being tied into bundles and carried to granaries for storage.

FARMING FAMILIES

This heavenly vision of the Field of Reeds was based on real, practical knowledge and experience. Most Egyptian families made their living by growing crops and raising animals on land made fertile by the Nile floods. They knew that if these floods failed, their crops would wither, and that they would go hungry and might even die. They learned how to manage the flood-waters by digging irrigation ditches and, after around 1500 BC, by using machines like the shaduf – a bucket fixed to a long pole that raised water from the river and poured it on to the fields.

CROPS AND ANIMALS

The most important field crops were grains, chiefly wheat and barley. These were planted after the land had been ploughed, in October or November, and were usually ready for harvest by March or April. If they stood in the fields for much longer, they risked being scorched by the hot summer sun.

Other food crops, such as onions, peas, beans, radishes and cabbages, were planted in small garden plots, which could be fenced to protect them from animals, and watered if the soil became dry.

Sesame (for oil) and

Right: An Egyptian farmer guides two oxen pulling a plough through the soil. Ploughing was men's work; women followed behind, scattering seeds.

Left: Picking grapes to crush to make wine. The Egyptians also made wine from other fruits that grew on their farms, including dates, figs and pomegranates. Drunkenness was allowed at feasts and at certain religious festivals.

But many farming families were able to produce enough, even after paying taxes and feeding their families, to exchange produce for small luxuries, such as bead necklaces and painted pottery, metal hunting knives and toys.

linen (used to make cloth) were also grown on Egyptian farms, along with palm trees (which produced dates) and vines. Ripe grapes from vines were carefully picked, then trampled underfoot to crush them and release the juice. This was collected into vats, left to ferment, then stored in huge pottery jars until it was ready to drink, as red or white wine. Sometimes, spices or honey were added, for extra sweetness and flavour.

Farm animals included ducks, geese, pigs, sheep and goats. In areas where there was plenty of grazing land, like the marshy Nile Delta region in

the north, farmers also kept cattle for milk, meat and leather. Oxen, the largest and heaviest farm animals, provided power to pull ploughs and carts. Donkeys were used to carry smaller, lighter loads. But camels, which thrive in the desert, were unknown in Egypt until around 800 BC.

PRESSURE TO PRODUCE

Egyptian farmers worked hard. But they did not get to enjoy all they produced. Most land was owned by pharaohs, rich noble families or temples. And most farmers and their families worked for them.

GONE FISHING

Many farmers kept ponds stocked with fish as a handy source of food. Others went fishing in the Nile, using traps or nets dragged between two boats (as shown in the Egyptian carving, below). Many poor families relied on fish to supplement their basic diet. But, for religious reasons, pharaohs and priests were not allowed to eat it at all – because a fish was the symbol of the evil god, Seth.

FAMILY LIFE

THE EGYPTIANS LOVED FAMILY LIFE. THEY HOPED FOR A HAPPY
MARRIAGE AND LOTS OF CHILDREN. FAMILIES SPENT MOST OF THEIR
FREE TIME TOGETHER – BOATING OR SWIMMING, SHARING MEALS
AND ENJOYING STORIES, SONGS, JOKES AND GAMES. BUT THE FAMILY
ALSO HAD A MUCH MORE PRACTICAL SIGNIFICANCE. GENERATIONS
WORKED TOGETHER TO EARN A LIVING, AND WHEN TIMES WERE
HARD, PEOPLE RELIED ON HELP FROM OTHER FAMILY MEMBERS.

Above: The Egyptians' main food
was bread. This was made from barley
and emmer wheat, their staple crops.
Bread could be baked in conical
moulds over open fires, or inside little
clay ovens.

GETTING MARRIED

Egyptian girls married young –
usually when they were about 12
years old. Often, their parents
chose a husband for them.
Egyptian boys waited until they
were about 20 before marrying.
By that age, they had learned
useful skills to help them
support a family. They were
often allowed to choose
their own bride.

Marriage was a private
arrangement, agreed
between a couple or
their families. The
Egyptians had no official
marriage ceremony, but
weddings were celebrated
with feasting, music,
dancing – and
sometimes a noisy,
cheerful procession
through the home

town or village of the groom.
The bride's family gave the
young couple useful gifts for
their new home, such as blankets,
or stocks of food for winter. It
was traditional for the groom to
give his wife a gift. If he was rich,
this might be a slave to help her
with her household tasks.

Left: Egyptian families
that were close and
loving in life hoped to
stay that way after
death, so they paid for
family statues – like this
one showing the dwarf
Seneb, a senior royal
official, and his wife and
children – to stand in
their tombs.

LEGAL RIGHTS

In law, the man was the head of each Egyptian household, but women were allowed to own property, run businesses and buy houses. They could also make wills and give independent evidence in court. The law allowed Egyptian men to have more than one wife,

for life, although this might not have been very long; few Egyptians lived above 40 years.

BABIES AND CHILDREN

The main purpose of marriage was to have children to carry on the family name. But childbirth held a high risk of death.

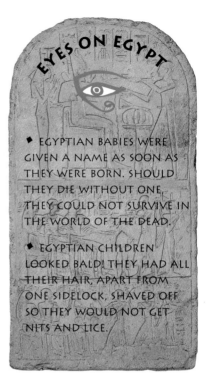

EYES ON EGYPT

• EGYPTIAN BABIES WERE GIVEN A NAME AS SOON AS THEY WERE BORN. SHOULD THEY DIE WITHOUT ONE, THEY COULD NOT SURVIVE IN THE WORLD OF THE DEAD.

• EGYPTIAN CHILDREN LOOKED BALD! THEY HAD ALL THEIR HAIR, APART FROM ONE SIDELOCK, SHAVED OFF SO THEY WOULD NOT GET NITS AND LICE.

Childhood was a time of danger too, with at least two out of 10 infants dying by the age of five, mainly from infectious diseases.

Egyptian children had simple toys including dolls, rattles and balls. Wealthy parents might send their sons to school, but most boys followed their fathers, learning to be farmers, craftsmen or scribes. Girls learnt household skills and childcare.

Egyptian sons were valued above daughters as only they could support their parents in old age and perform the special funeral ceremonies that ensured continued life in the Next World.

but a wife could only have one husband, and was expected to stay faithful to him. If she did not, she could be put to death. If a couple could not live happily together, they both had the right to ask for a divorce, and women could have a share of the family property. But most couples remained married

Above: Who's winning? Senet was a favourite Egyptian game played on a board with counters of wood or clay. Players threw dice to decide how many squares to move. Senet also had a religious meaning; it symbolised the struggle between good and evil.

Right: A typical family home, recreated in miniature as a container for food offerings left outside tombs. Most ordinary Egyptians lived in low-rise, flat-roofed houses like this.

LOOKING GOOD

ANCIENT EGYPTIANS LIKED TO LOOK GOOD. CLOTHES, JEWELLERY AND MAKE-UP WERE IMPORTANT TO BOTH WOMEN AND MEN. CLOTHES SENT OUT IMPORTANT MESSAGES. SOFT, PLEATED ROBES, AN ELABORATE HAIRSTYLE, SMOOTH, PERFUMED SKIN AND GOLDEN JEWELLERY TOLD THE WORLD THAT THE WEARER WAS RICH, ELEGANT AND FASTIDIOUS. THE EGYPTIANS ALSO BELIEVED THAT CLOTHES AND JEWELS DECORATED WITH MAGIC SYMBOLS HAD PROTECTIVE POWERS.

Above: A woman (centre) hands perfumed wax to her friend, to scent her wig. Egyptians used oils and fats mixed with sweet-smelling resin from plants to soften and perfume their skin. They also made strange mixtures from roasted ostrich eggs, tamarisk and tortoiseshell to remove body odour.

SIMPLE STYLES

The basic design of Egyptian clothes changed very little over the centuries – a long, loose tunic for women, and a knee-length kilt for men. Both were made of linen, and were usually pale fawn colour or white – because linen fibres are very difficult to dye.

In winter, and after dark, when it could get chilly, men and women wrapped woollen blankets around their shoulders for warmth.

Shoes as such did not exist. People would normally go barefoot or wear flat, open sandals made of leather or plaited rushes.

Right: A delicate earring made around 1500 BC of gold, carnelian, turquoise and lapis lazuli.

PALACE FASHIONS

Among rich women, fashions did slowly change. Until about 1650 BC, long straight robes were fashionable – sometimes worn with a net over-dress, which would often be ornately decorated with beads.

After 1500 BC, fashionable clothes became much fuller and looser, and were often rather ostentatiously trimmed with fringes or pleats.

MAKING UP

As well as looking attractive, the Egyptians believed that make-up protected their eyes from the glare of the sun and from diseases carried by flies. Bright green eyeliner, made from malachite (a semi-precious stone) crushed and mixed with water, was fashionable in early Egyptian times. Later, glittery grey eyeliner made from lead (shown, left, on this statue of Tutankhamun) was more popular. Eye make-up was worn by both women and men. Women also used powdered ochre (a red mineral) to colour their cheeks, or they mixed it with oil to make lipstick.

NO CLOTHES AT ALL

Children, servants, labourers and slaves are often shown nude in Egyptian statues and paintings; clothes got in the way of hard, physical work and children's games. But when they did wear clothes all Egyptians, even poor families, liked them to be clean. Professional washermen made a living scrubbing clothes with harsh, salty soap beside the Nile.

Left: Fashionable men and women who wore heavy wigs had their heads shaved, because it was cooler and more comfortable.

BIG WIGS

Hairstyles also changed. Before around 2000 BC, Egyptians wore their hair short. Then for about the next 500 years, shoulder-length hair was fashionable, and wealthy people wore heavy, braided wigs decorated with jewels or beads. From 1500 BC, two very different styles were popular – short, curly or braided wigs, modelled on the haircuts of Nubian soldiers, or long, tangled ringlets. Baldness and grey hair were both very unfashionable. Remedies for baldness included rubbing all sorts of curious mixtures, such as blended lion, hippo, cat and snake fat on the scalp to make the hair grow.

MADE BY HAND

Whatever the style, all Egyptian clothes were made slowly and painstakingly by hand, and were therefore very expensive. A woman's tunic could cost as much as a goat. Most linen and woollen cloth was spun and woven by women, working at home or in special workshops – crowded rooms, almost like factories, on big estates owned by temples or noble families. Workers all had their own particular skills. Each woman finished her own particular task, then passed it on to others further along the production line for the next stage.

Below: Rich, powerful people employed skilled servants to help them bathe and dress. Ordinary people just washed in the River Nile.

FOOD AND FEASTING

THE ANCIENT EGYPTIANS ENJOYED THEIR FOOD. SHARING MEALS WITH FRIENDS AND NEIGHBOURS WAS A PLEASANT SOCIAL DUTY, AND EVERYONE LOOKED FORWARD TO SPECIAL FEASTS. BUT IT WAS BAD MANNERS TO BE GREEDY. ONE SCRIBE WARNED, 'A CUP OF WATER WILL SATISFY YOUR THIRST... A MOUTHFUL OF VEGETABLES WILL STRENGTHEN YOUR HEART... IT IS VILE TO LET YOUR BELLY HUNGER FOR MORE FOOD AFTER MEAL TIMES HAVE PASSED.'

EYES ON EGYPT

IN 1962, ARCHAEOLOGISTS FOUND THE FOLLOWING FOODS IN AN OLD WOMAN'S TOMB AT SAQQARA DATING FROM 2800 BC. THE FOOD WAS CAREFULLY ARRANGED READY FOR A FEAST IN THE NEXT WORLD, AND WAS AMAZINGLY WELL-PRESERVED:

● BREAD ● BARLEY ● CHEESE ● PORRIDGE ● ROAST FISH ● PIGEON STEW ● ROAST QUAIL ● KIDNEYS AND BEEF ● STEWED FIGS AND FRESH BERRIES ● HONEY CAKES ● WINE

Left: These pottery jars were used for carrying water and for storing grain, wine and honey.

Right: A woman servant using a saddle-quern. Grains of wheat were tipped on to the slab, then the roller was pushed back and forth to grind them into rough flour.

ONE MAIN MEAL

Egyptian families ate only one main meal each day, around noon, with just a light snack for breakfast and at supper time. The most important Egyptian foods were bread, beer and vegetables. These were sometimes paid as wages. Workmen building royal tombs were given ten loaves of bread each, every day, and two jugs of beer – but this had to feed their wives and children as well.

GRITTY BREAD

Bread was made from wheat grains ground into a rough flour, using a slab of stone with a stone roller, called a 'saddle quern'. Bakers – usually women – mixed this flour with water and shaped it into round, flat loaves, which they then baked in very hot clay ovens.

Egyptian bread was tasty when fresh, but terribly gritty. It contained sand blown in from the desert and sharp little fragments from quern-stones. As a result, most Egyptian people's teeth were chipped and worn.

THICK BEER

Beer was made from barley flavoured with dates, honey or spices. It was so thick and soupy that it had to be sucked up through a wooden tube fitted with a strainer. This trapped scum from the brewing process and any insects that had fallen in. Egyptian beer was not very strong, but it was nourishing and tasted sweet, so it was often given to children.

RAW FISH AND GARLIC

Favourite vegetables included onions, lettuce,

Above: Women entertainers at a feast. Many Egyptian songs encouraged guests to enjoy themselves as much as they could – because life was short!

cucumbers, leeks and garlic. All were eaten raw. The Egyptians also liked fresh fruit, especially melons, grapes and figs. Egyptian farmers grew chickpeas and beans, which were cooked in clay pots balanced on top of bread-ovens. Many families – in towns as well as on farms – kept livestock including chickens and goats, to provide eggs, milk and cheese. Young men went hunting in the desert and fishing in the River Nile. According to one Greek traveller, the Egyptians often ate fish raw, either salted or dried in the sun. (There was not much wood available in Egypt for cooking fires.) They trapped small birds to eat raw but always cooked other meat, such as beef, goat or mutton by stewing or roasting over an open fire.

FOOD FOR FEASTS

Ordinary families ate meat only a few times each year, at feasts on important occasions, such as religious festivals. Rich families could afford meat more often to feed themselves and their guests. Favourite treats included steaks from specially-reared cattle with tender, fatty flesh. Wealthy families also enjoyed other luxuries, such as honey-cakes, fresh figs, pomegranates, almonds and red wine. Entertaining was an important task for pharaohs and powerful dignitaries. It rewarded their supporters and displayed their power. They paid for singers, dancers, acrobats and musicians to entertain their guests at feasts, and for servant-girls to welcome them with garlands of sweet-smelling flowers and cones of scented wax to wear in their hair.

Left: Beer was made by stirring barley and wheat with water in big pottery jars, then leaving the mixture in a warm place to ferment. It became slightly alcoholic, and was ready to drink in a few days.

TRADE, TRIBUTE AND TRANSPORT

EGYPTIAN PHARAOHS CLAIMED TO BE 'RULERS OF ALL THE WORLD'. THIS WAS NOT TRUE. EGYPT WAS CERTAINLY A LARGE COUNTRY, AND, FOR MANY CENTURIES, BETWEEN 1500 BC AND 1000 BC, RULED A WIDE EMPIRE STRETCHING FROM SYRIA TO SUDAN. BUT THE EGYPTIANS KNEW VERY WELL THAT OTHER POWERFUL PEOPLES LIVED BEYOND THEIR FRONTIERS. WHAT DID THEY MEAN BY MAKING SUCH A PROUD, EXAGGERATED CLAIM?

RICHER AND STRONGER

Boasting that they ruled the world was the Egyptians' way of saying that they were richer and stronger than any of their neighbours. Egypt's riches came from taxes paid by its large population – and also from trade. Its wealth and large army made it strong enough to defend its frontiers from attack, to invade and take control of nearby lands and to demand tribute (valuable goods) from conquered countries.

LOCAL AND LONG DISTANCE

Egyptian families produced many essential items for themselves, including food and clothing.

Above: Nubians, from Sudan, carrying tribute, including heavy gold rings. Egypt traded with Nubia for over 1000 years before sending soldiers and building a chain of fortresses to take control of its rich resources around 1950 BC.

But they traded surplus farm produce, such as meat, eggs and wine at local markets. All trading was done by barter – coins were not introduced to Egypt until about 600 BC. Before then, merchants set out displays of goods for sale, and buyers offered items in exchange until both sides were satisfied with the deal.

In towns, there were shops and stalls selling a much wider range of goods, including some brought by traders from distant lands. In the ruins of ancient Egyptian towns archaeologists have found fragments of pots made by Minoan workers on the island of Crete. Egyptian merchants also travelled long distances to trade with other countries both in Africa and around the shores of the Mediterranean Sea.

GOVERNMENT BUSINESS

The best, most trustworthy traders were known as shwtyw and worked for the Egyptian

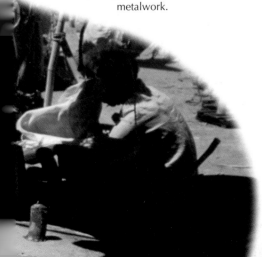

Left: Villagers barter home-made cloth and home-grown vegetables at local markets for goods made by craft-workers specialising in furniture, pottery, jewellery and metalwork.

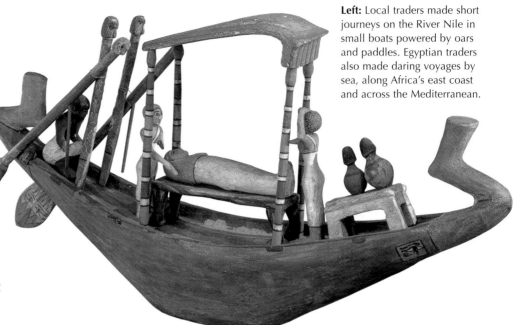

Left: Local traders made short journeys on the River Nile in small boats powered by oars and paddles. Egyptian traders also made daring voyages by sea, along Africa's east coast and across the Mediterranean.

government, and handled important international business deals. Some rulers, such as Queen Hatshepsut, sent government traders on special missions to bring back rare and valuable goods from the land of Punt (Eritrea). They returned with gold, ivory, ebony, myrrh (a sweet-smelling plant gum, burned as incense), pet apes and hunting dogs. Chief priest Herihor sent a trading fleet to the port of Byblos, in Syria, to bring back top-quality cedarwood for his royal palace, because timber-producing trees did not grow well in Egypt's hot, dry climate.

TREASURES AND TRIBUTE

Trusted shwty merchants also carried presents, including real gold statues, from pharaohs to foreign rulers. These gifts were a sign of friendship – and a demonstration of Egypt's wealth

and power. In return, pharaohs expected to receive gifts of equal – or greater – value, such as perfume, ivory, precious stones and works of art. These treasures, together with tribute of slaves, copper and leopard-skins, sent to Egypt by conquered peoples, made Egypt the richest country in the region.

Above: Pharaohs, rich merchants, foreign envoys and other important people travelled in litters – seats fitted with shady curtains and carried shoulder-high by slaves.

WARRIORS AT WAR

EGYPTIAN CIVILISATION WAS BASED ON PEACE, NOT WAR. MOST OF EGYPT'S RULERS VALUED TREASURES, TEMPLES AND TOMBS MORE THAN MILITARY GLORY. NONETHELESS, FROM AROUND 1900 BC, THEY KEPT A LARGE, WELL-ORGANISED ARMY READY TO FIGHT. SOME WARLIKE PHARAOHS, SUCH AS TUTHMOSIS III AND RAMESES II, LED EGYPTIAN SOLDIERS TO CONQUER OTHER LANDS.

Above: Four bows and four quivers of arrows. Composite bows were constructed from layers of birch-wood, bulls' tendons and goats' horns, bonded with fish glue. Arrows were made of reeds, with stone or metal tips.

PHARAOHS AND PROFESSIONALS

The Egyptian army was the largest in the ancient world. By around 1250 BC, it had over 100,000 men. According to ancient tradition, the ruling pharaoh, or his son, was chief commander. But some pharaohs were not capable of leading armies into battle. Some, such as Tutankhamun, were too young, others, like Akhenaten, were more interested in peaceful pursuits. Pharaohs who did not fight relied on skilled professionals to lead their armies. Officers came mostly from families with a military tradition. Sons followed their fathers into the army and learned from their experiences in battle and on the march.

Some ordinary soldiers were also paid professionals, but most were conscripts, who were forced to fight. Men and boys from farming, trading, or craftworking families were commanded to join the army by government scribes, who kept lists of suitable recruits in each village and town. If any man tried to hide, armed guards came to his house and dragged him away. For these untrained men, joining the army could be a terrifying experience. Few had ever left their homes and families before, or moved so far away. They did not know whether they would ever return home or see their loved ones again.

Left: Soldiers trained for battle by practising hand-to-hand combat with daggers, spears and their favourite weapons – long-handled battle-axes with curved bronze blades that could slice through flesh and bone.

ON THE MARCH

Once war had been declared, the pharaoh's army set off to the battlegrounds on foot. Soldiers marching to war could cover 24 km/15 miles each day. But men on the march often collapsed from dehydration or exhaustion. In hot desert lands, each soldier needed 9 litres/17 pints of water every day, and this could be difficult to find. Each man also carried his kit with him weighing up to 27 kg/60 lb – a crippling burden for a weak or injured soldier.

On long journeys, armies built camps for shelter arranged in a neat grid pattern surrounded by a fence of wooden shields. But marching armies and their camps were always vulnerable to attack. Enemy troops ambushed hot, tired, thirsty Egyptian soldiers. They also poisoned local wells (by dropping in the rotting carcasses of dead sheep) and shot blazing arrows into enemy army camps, setting them on fire.

RICH REWARDS

Men who survived harsh army life received land and farm animals on retirement. Some were even given enemy captives as slaves. Soldiers could also claim a pension of grain. Slaves who had served in the army were rewarded by being set free.

Above: This model, found in a tomb, shows a column of soldiers carrying shields and spears. An army marching through the desert stirred up dust which choked and blinded the men.

Below: An Egyptian army on the move. The officers wear armour and some ride in horse-drawn chariots. All soldiers carry a shield and a spear.

ON THE BATTLEFIELD

EGYPTIAN ARMIES USED TWO DIFFERENT TACTICS TO DEFEAT THEIR ENEMIES – SIEGES AND PITCHED BATTLES. IN A SIEGE, EGYPTIAN SOLDIERS SURROUNDED AN ENEMY CITY AND CUT OFF SUPPLIES OF FOOD AND WATER UNTIL THE CITIZENS SURRENDERED OR STARVED TO DEATH. IN A PITCHED BATTLE, THEY MARCHED TOWARDS ENEMY TROOPS AND CONFRONTED THEM FACE-TO-FACE.

Above: Painted stone-carving showing the strong arm of Pharaoh Rameses II (ruled 1279–1213 BC) holding enemy captives by the hair. They come from three neighbouring lands invaded by Egypt: Nubia (Sudan), Libya and Syria.

FIGHTING ON FOOT

Egyptian foot-soldiers were armed with wooden spears and long-handled battle-axes. The heaviest axes could even cut through armour. Foot-soldiers also used daggers and throwsticks to stab or stun their enemies, but the deadliest Egyptian weapons were powerful composite bows. These fired arrows to hit targets over 175 metres away.

SIDE BY SIDE

On the battlefield, enemy armies arranged themselves in close formation, with rows of soldiers standing shoulder to shoulder, protecting each other with overlapping shields. Then they marched forwards until soldiers at the front of each army were fighting, hand-to-hand, with daggers, axes and spears. As men in the front line were killed or injured, more soldiers moved up from behind to take their place.

This method of fighting was very frightening. One ancient Egyptian writer described it this way: 'The enemy advances, surrounds the soldier with missiles, and all is chaos. He is told, "Quick, forward, valiant soldier! Win yourself a good name!" He does not know what to do. His body is weak, his legs fail him.'

Faced with this onslaught, troops on one side or the

EYES ON EGYPT

- BOYS COULD BE FORCED TO JOIN THE ARMY WHEN THEY WERE ONLY 10 YEARS OLD.

- AFTER A BATTLE, SOLDIERS CUT OFF ONE HAND FROM EACH DEAD ENEMY FIGHTER. SCRIBES THEN RECORDED THE TOTAL NUMBER COLLECTED.

- PRIESTS AND MUMMY MAKERS ACCOMPANIED ARMIES TO PRESERVE THE BODIES OF THE RICH.

Right: Pharaohs and elite warriors rode in fast, horse-drawn chariots. They charged towards the enemy, shooting arrows to cause panic among foot-soldiers. Chariots were also used by scouts, who rode ahead of the army to spy out the land.

Left: Foot-soldiers relied on shields made of wood and leather to ward off deadly blows from battle-axes. Army commanders also wore bronze helmets and body armour, a luxury not afforded by ordinary fighting men.

Below: Gold 'flies of valour' were awarded like medals to soldiers who fought bravely in battle.

other soon panicked, broke out of close formation, and ran away. But, as soldiers scattered to try and find safety, they were trampled by enemy chariots and shot at by enemy archers. Most men who died in battle were killed as they ran away.

Many more died in the days after a battle. Skilled doctors working for the Egyptian army pioneered the treatment of battle injuries – setting broken bones and stopping flesh-wounds from getting infected. For instance, they cauterised (sealed) wounds with a hot knife to stop them bleeding, used honey mixed with salt as an antiseptic and even invented an early form of sticking plaster, made from bandages and gum, to keep wounds both clean and protected. But even so, historians have estimated that one out of every four soldiers injured in battle did not survive.

THE BATTLE OF MEGIDDO

Above: Tuthmosis III. After being kept off the throne by his stepmother for over 20 years, he is keen to prove himself as a pharaoh and a warrior.

Below: Tuthmosis and his soldiers prepare to enter the defeated city of Megiddo. As the pharaoh advanced Syrian princes and nobles sent out groups of children, carrying weapons, jewellery and other treasures, as a sign of their surrender.

Queen Hatshepsut was an extraordinary woman. For over 20 years, she ruled Egypt on behalf of her stepson, Pharaoh Tuthmosis III, refusing to let him take part in government during her lifetime. When she died in 1458 BC Tuthmosis lost no time in making plans for action. He wanted to equal the achievements of his warlike grandfather, Pharaoh Tuthmosis I, who won famous victories in Nubia (now Sudan) and Mesopotamia (now Iraq).

Less than one year after Hatshepsut died, Tuthmosis set out on his first campaign. He aimed to end a rebellion in Syria, which his grandfather had forced to pay tribute many years ago. The rebels were led by the prince of Kadesh, a Syrian city-state supported by the powerful Mitanni people – Egypt's enemies – from their homeland further north. The rebel armies were camped close to the well-defended city of Megiddo, which controlled important long-distance trade routes linking the Mediterranean Sea and Syria and with the Persian Gulf.

As soon as harvest was safely gathered in, Tuthmosis sent scribes to the countryside, conscripting young men to

Above: A lucky escape! This Egyptian soldier wears a lucky wadjet amulet, shaped like the eye of the god Horus, to protect him from sudden death.

join his army. The new soldiers had no choice. By law, the pharaoh could force them to serve for as long as he wished. Many recruits did not survive the tough training, the long marches through the desert, or the bloody battles against desperate enemies.

By spring 1457 BC the army was ready – it totalled over 10,000 men. It took them months to reach Megiddo, and then Tuthmosis faced a difficult decision. He could advance slowly, but safely, from either the north or the south, or he could make a rapid, risky move, and march straight ahead through a narrow mountain pass. Ignoring advice from his more experienced army commanders, Tuthmosis chose to make the surprise attack through the pass.

His plan worked brilliantly – at first. The Egyptians charged the enemy camp, slashing and stabbing with battleaxes and spears. But then they stopped to plunder the bodies of dead Syrians, giving others the chance to flee to safety behind Megiddo's strong gates and walls. The pharaoh was furious. He knew that he had lost his chance to capture Megiddo in a single fierce fight. In fact, it took

over seven months to force the city's surrender – and for Tuthmosis to win his first victory.

We know about Tuthmosis because a young scribe, Tjeneni, wrote down details of his battles, becoming the first war-reporter in the world. Tuthmosis gave orders for Tjeneni's text to be carved in hieroglyphs on the walls of the great temple of Amun at Karnak. Later, all statues and paintings recording the life of Hatshepsut were destroyed.

Pharaoh Tuthmosis III is remembered today as a great warrior pharaoh. For seventeen years he led his armies on campaigns to the east and north, and conquered more land than his famous grandfather. By the time Tuthmosis died in 1425 BC, the Egyptians proudly claimed, 'Egypt extends as far as the circuit of the sun.'

Above: Syrians fleeing the Egyptian attack climbed into Megiddo using ropes let down by women on top of the city walls. The prince of Kadesh had to be hauled up over the wall by his clothes!

Below: After the first battle-charge by charioteers firing arrows, Syrian and Egyptian soldiers fight face to face, with battleaxes, spears and swords.

AN EMPIRE IN DECLINE

FOR OVER 3000 YEARS, EGYPT WAS HOME TO A RICH AND SPLENDID CIVILISATION REACHING ITS PEAK DURING THE NEW KINGDOM 1550–1069 BC. EGYPT'S CRAFTWORKERS CREATED SPLENDID BUILDINGS AND SUMPTUOUS TREASURES, ITS PHARAOHS WON GREAT VICTORIES IN BATTLE AND EGYPTIAN TRADERS TRAVELLED TO DISTANT AFRICAN, ASIAN AND MEDITERRANEAN LANDS.

Above: Alexander the Great (lived 356–323 BC). After taking control of Egypt, he marched east, to conquer a vast empire.

INVADERS

However, after this 'golden age', Egyptian power began to decline, and Egypt was attacked by hostile peoples from the north and east. The country was a rich prize for any invader and, as it produced no more strong pharaohs to command its

Below: A street in Saqqara at the time of the Ptolemies. Under their rule, 323–30 BC, Greek coins and other aspects of Greek art and architecture were adopted across Egypt.

Above: Cleopatra VII (ruled 51–30 BC), was clever and charming, but could not stop Roman invasion. Egypt became 'the granary (grain-store) of the empire' – a backwater producing much-needed food for other Roman-controlled lands.

army, control ambitious local governors, or fight off enemy attack, it was an easy target.

For a while, Egypt's religion, culture and way of life continued as before, but in 671 BC, Assyrian warriors invaded and conquered the northern half of the country. Then, in 525 BC, all Egypt became part of the mighty Persian empire, after Emperor Cambyses II led an army across the Nile.

In 332 BC, yet another group of invaders, Macedonians from the north of Greece, seized control, led by Alexander the Great – their ruthless but brilliant young king. Alexander and his army soon marched on, but he left one of his generals, Ptolemy, in charge of Egypt, founding a new dynasty that would last 300 years.

THE PTOLEMIES

Ptolemy and his descendants ruled Egypt well at first, but later became foolish, selfish and quarrelsome. They also faced a fearsome new threat – the fast-growing empire of Rome, whose soldiers were conquering new lands in Europe, North Africa and the Middle East. In 58 BC, Egyptian ruler Ptolemy XII made an alliance with Rome, hoping to fend off attack for a while. But the Egyptian people were so angry with him that he was forced to flee.

EGYPT'S QUEEN

After several years of family feuding, Ptolemy XII's daughter, Cleopatra, became queen of Egypt in 51 BC. She used her beauty to fight against Rome, pursuing dangerous love affairs with the empire's commanders, Julius Caesar and Mark Antony. But even this daring strategy could not stop the invaders' advance – in AD 31, Roman general Octavian marched on Egypt. Realising that she could not save her country, Cleopatra committed suicide rather than be captured by Roman soldiers.

RULED BY ROME

After Cleopatra's death in AD 30, Egypt became a province of Rome and was ruled by Roman governors for 500 years. The Ptolemies' capital city, Alexandria, continued to be a great centre of learning and trade, but Egypt's power and glory slowly faded away.

Egypt became a tourist destination for people from neighbouring lands, such as Greece, who came to admire its splendid monuments and colourful religious festivals. And people still flock today to marvel at the wonders of Ancient Egypt.

Above: Some Egyptian customs continued after Roman invasion. This mummy was made around AD 100 using traditional Egyptian techniques, but it is decorated with a lifelike portrait in the Roman style.

GLOSSARY

Alexandria The capital of Egypt in Greek and Roman times.

Amun-Re Powerful god of Thebes associated with the sun. Also referred to as Ra.

amulet A protective charm.

Anubis The jackal-headed god of embalming and cemeteries.

ankh Cross with looped top. A symbol of life.

Apis bull The god Ptah in animal shape.

Book of the Dead A collection of magic spells to protect the dead in the Next World.

branded Marked by using a hot iron to burn skin and flesh.

criosphinx Monster shaped like a lion with a ram's head.

delta Marshy land where a river flows into the sea.

demotic Egyptian script, based on hieroglyphs, that could be written quickly.

Deshret (Red Land) Egyptian word for desert.

dynasty Ruling family.

Field of Reeds A pleasant, peaceful place in the Next World.

flint A hard stone that can be chipped to make a sharp edge.

hieratic A way of writing Egyptian hieroglyphs on papyrus. Used for important documents.

heiroglyphs Egyptian writing that used picture-symbols.

Horus Hawk-headed scribe god.

incense Substance such as frankincense that gives off a sweet-smelling smoke when burned. Used in holy places like temples.

inscriptions Writing on stone.

Isis Goddess sister-wife of Osiris.

ka Life force.

Kemet (Black Land) Egyptian word for fertile soil.

kiosk Small temple.

lapis lazuli Semi-precious blue stone used to decorate jewellery and other objects.

litter Small bed, with curtains, used to carry important people.

magistrates Junior judges.

mastaba Early Egyptian tomb, shaped like a block or a bench.

meret Egyptian word meaning 'unfree'.

necropolis 'City of the Dead'. Greek word for burial ground used to describe Egyptian cemeteries.

notaries Scribes who have studied the law.

Nubia Land south of Egypt; present-day Sudan.

Osiris God of the dead. Brother of and husband of Isis.

ostraca Small pieces of pottery, used to write notes on.

pharaoh (Great House) Egyptian king.

Punt Land south of Egypt; probably pesent-day Eritrea.

resin Gum (dried sap) produced by plants.

Saqqara Holy city on the edge of the desert near Memphis.

sarcophagus (Flesh Eater) Greek word for a stone coffin.

scribes Educated men who served as government and temple officials.

shabti Statuettes placed in tombs to help the dead in the afterlife.

shrine A holy place; the holiest part of a temple.

shwty (pl. shwtyw) Trained, trusted merchant who acted as international messenger for the government.

solar bark A mythical boat that sailed through the sky, carrying the spirits of dead pharaohs.

tendon Strong, stretchy tissue that connects muscle and bone.

tithes Share of produce, paid as a kind of tax.

venom Poison.

Vizier Chief minister, Prime Minister.

INDEX

ACKNOWLEDGMENTS AND PICTURE CREDITS

The publishers would like to thank the following for providing photographs and granting permission to reproduce copyright material:

Ancient Art & Architecture Collection 12t, 13br, 19tl, 31m, 38t **Ancient Egypt Picture Library** 8b, 25t, 35, 39b, 43br, 50t **The Art Archive** 59tl **The Art Archive/Dagli Orti** 14b, 15b, 34b, 40t, 43t, 46tl, **The Art Archive/Archaeological Museum Naples/Dagli Orti** 58t, **The Art Archive/Egyptian Museum Cairo/Dagli Orti** 6, 34t, 41br, 46tr, 46b, 54t, **British Museum** 22l, 23bl, 26r, 27 (all), 28b, 42-43b, 51t, 55tr, 59r, **Werner Forman Archive** 9t, 14t, 23tr, 28t, 44bl, 45b, 48bl, 49t, **Jilly MacLeod** 23br, **Science Photo Library** 10-11b, 11br **Archivio White Star/Araldo de Luca** 53t

('Eyes on Egypt' panels on pp.13, 19, 24, 32, 45, 48 & 54 show a funerary stela of Nebnehehabsu courtesy of **Birmingham Museums & Art Gallery**)

All other photographs courtesy of **Wall to Wall Productions**

While every effort has been made to trace and acknowledge all copyright holders, we would like to apologise should any omissions have been made.

Key to abbreviations: t (top); b (bottom); m (middle); l (left); r (right)